TRL

Since I don't have network or cable TV at home, I tend to watch a lot of documentaries, educational flicks, and instructional videos. The very best of these non-fiction films are as entertaining as the best of Hollywood blockbusters. Many true films are wonderful, but move in a different direction from fiction. And most true films are solidly informative, and useful like a tool.

I list here 100 great true films. These are the best non-fiction films I've found for general interest. I define true films as documentaries, educational films, instructional how-to's, and what the British call factuals – a non-fiction visual account.

In contrast to the fiction that most movies are, true films offer authentic plot twists, real characters, and truth stranger than fiction. They aim to both entertain and to inform – a powerful combo. It is no puzzle that true films are enjoying an expanding audience and rising prestige.

I've watched and endorse all but a few of the films recommended here. All the unsigned reviews in this book are mine. Two other documentary fans have suggested and reviewed a few films I have not seen. Their initials follow their reviews: Jim Daly (JD) and Richard Kadrey (RK).

As dogged as I have been in tracking down great true films, I have seen only a fraction of the estimated 40,000 that have been made. So I am ready for more. I intend to keep this booklet updated with future editions. If you know of an amazing true film that I've missed please recommend it: kk@kk.org.

Where to get the films:

For too long true films have been hard to find, appearing only fleetingly in theaters, or projected in school classrooms on expensive 16mm prints, or hidden on back shelves at video rental places. Now DVDs and websites are rapidly enlarging the availability of true films; their prices continue to drop, and their distribution increases.

However many great true films are still not easily seen. The British make fantastic factuals that are shown a few times on BBC and then mothballed. A lot of older documentaries are still not released on DVD or tape. Many that do make it to VHS are priced very expensively according to the old model of scarce film prints. Distributors may charge $300 to purchase a tape, and $100 merely to rent. I view this as an ideal strategy to prevent as many people as possible from seeing a film.

Happily, more and more recent documentaries are being released to a receptive public at consumer prices. Even better, a growing number are also carried by the emerging online DVD subscription services, like Netflix (which carries 1,200 documentaries), Greencine (also 1,200), and even WalMart (which lists only a few hundred true films).

I recommend here only those great and worthwhile titles that are available on tape or DVD at consumer prices. I indicate first whether a film is rentable from Netflix, and then if it is purchasable from Amazon. If neither of those options are available, I will then list an alternative source.

Shopping information changes rapidly so I'm trying to keep the ordering information for each film current on my website, at www.truefilms.com. Check there if you are having trouble finding something.

If a film is not found for sale on the used-item section of Amazon, you should check Ebay, which carries a surprising number of used videos and DVDs.

I am a huge fan of the film subscription service Netflix (www.netflix.com). Their library of 25,000 films (including 1,200 true films) is now my library via my mailbox. The long list of films I want to see is kept on my computer; the films come as DVD disks in the mail; I always hold 3 and I send them back in the same envelope (no postage and no late fees) whenever I am done. The service is amazingly fast, incredibly intelligent, inexpensive, and the best way to try out documentaries in a low risk way (it costs you nothing to return a disk unviewed). Give them a try (each film is linked at my True Film site). If there is a true film you want to see that they don't have, ask them to order it.

A similar service that specializes in indie productions is GreenCine (www.greencine.com) which has 18,000 films in total; I have not found a service specializing in true films yet, but I expect to see one someday soon.

Don't forget your local public library either. It is not uncommon for libraries in one region to pool their videos into a decent video library, yours for the asking. Even the saddest video rental store should also carry at least a dozen of these titles.

Enjoy. And let me know which films you like the best. Even better, tell me about one I missed.

-- Kevin Kelly
Winter 2004

1900 House
Frontier House

Take an ordinary middle class family of the year 2000 and make them live for 6 months like an ordinary middle class family of the year 1900. The London-based producers succeed in this transformation by getting every detail of Victorian domestic life exactly right and complete. There is no escape from this time machine. No shampoo, either. The edited 6-hour result is deep, instructive, and totally riveting. Kids who hate history are mesmerized by it. Because it is so visual and visceral, it changed the discussion of chores and gender roles in our household. Better than 100 essays, this video series reveals the notion of progress. It is now my favorite history "book."

The success of *1900 House* spawned *Frontier House*, a parallel experiment that transfers the conceit to the edge of Montana in 1893 during homesteading days. It ups the challenge by requiring three families to build their homesteads and raise all their own food while sticking to period tools and the lifestyle of pioneers. Instead of cooperating, they compete against each other – good drama for watching. There is probably no greater persuader of women's inequality than this pair of films. The guys loved being pioneers, while the women and girls were imprisoned by it. If I had to choose only one to see, I'd go with *Frontier House*. There's more going on, more intra-personal weirdness, more learning and more failures.

1900 House
1999, 240 min

Frontier House
2002, 360 min

Netflix
Amazon

9/11

By fantastic coincidence two young French filmmakers were documenting the life of a New York firehouse for several months when the Twin Towers were stuck by planes. They not only caught the second plane on film, they then followed the same firefighters into the towers and by luck they returned with the most amazing inside look at the hellish events as the towers burned and crashed. In addition to the expected horror, the film also has its own drama because you are waiting – like the other firemen in the station – to find out who did not return from the collapse. The footage is heroic and astounding and heartbreaking. I experienced a huge sense of emotional closure by watching the film because I now felt I had some idea of what happened in the offices; I felt I was there. This documentary guarantees you a journey you won't forget.

By Jules Gedeon Naudet and James Hanlon
2002
120 min

Netflix
Amazon

Amazing Grace

The simplest are sometimes the best. This documentary is about one song, "Amazing Grace." An amazing lot can be seen through this four-stanza song. Bill Moyers follows the origins and evolution of one of the world's most famous hymns. It is part music history, part African-American history, and part song itself.

By Billl Moyers
1999
70 min

Amazon

American Movie

Some people find this documentary depressing because it is about a man trapped by dreams larger than his resources. A 30-year-old slacker in a dead prairie town in Wisconsin dreams of making a horror flic. He has no money, no skills, no equipment, and no clue. Using beer money earned from delivery newspapers, he bullies his astoundingly drug-addled friends into acting while he ineptly directs, often getting his elderly mom to help out as incompetent gripper. These scenes are very funny. For years his film is only talk, while he lounges in front of a TV and fights with his girl friend in a trailer park or tries to wheedle money from his senile uncle. All riveting in their reality. You are utterly convinced his film will never be made. Yet scene by crazy scene, filmed in his kitchen or car over the seasons, he finally completes his non-masterpiece. When finished, his friends shrug like zombies. Was it worth the incredible determination it took given his situation? He is the only one who thinks so. I found his hurdles to be real, and his delusion of success inspiring.

By Chris Smith
1999
104 min

Netflix
Amazon

Atomic Cafe

No need to mock nuclear power and atomic weapons when the promoters do it so well themselves. This brilliant compilation of mostly government-funded atomic propaganda films is very campy. Imagine a nuclear version of *Reefer Madness.* (RK)

By Jayne Loader and Pierce Rafferty
1982
88 min

Netflix
Amazon

Baka: The People of the Forest

This is one of the all-time great visual anthropology pieces. It took the filmmakers two years to settle into a village of Pygmies and six months of warming up before they even began filming. All this care transforms exotic natives into next-door people. My favorite part is when the little boy tells his parent he wants them to send his newborn brother back from wherever it was that he came. Noble savages, this ain't.

$18
Available from Click4Stuff
http://store.yahoo.com/ggroup/bakpeopoffor.html

By Phil Agland
1990
100 min

Baraka

A cinematic poem celebrating the human relation to the eternal. Not a word is spoken, but every person alive in the twenty-four countries this was filmed in would understand it. It's about Us on Earth Now. It's the first truly sacred film I've seen (best viewed in DVD on as large a screen as possible). Next time they send a disc into space to be viewed by aliens, this is the disc they should send.

By Ron Fricke
1992
104 min

Netflix
Amazon

Blood in the Face

A Day in the Life of White Supremacist America, shot in Michigan in 1991. This film captures both the collective power of racist groups and the frightening banality of the beliefs of the groups' individual members. (RK)

By Kevin Rafferty and James Ridgeway
1991
78 min

Amazon

Blue Planet: The Deep

You want life weird and strange? It's in the deep a mile down. You don't know life at all until you've met these spectacularly different creatures. I mean way different. Totally bizarre, totally awesome. Guaranteed to alter your consciousness. The filmmaking is superb and jaw-dropping. The entire series is wonderful, but if you merely want a wholly unexpected view of "whats' down there," the disk you want is Disc 2: *The Deep* and *Open Ocean* where life emerges different.

Narrated by David Attenborough
2001
98 min

Netflix
Amazon

Bob Dylan: Don't Look Back

The iconographic rockumentary, filmed before rock musicians had handlers. This peek inside the head of a very young Bob Dylan is disturbing and exhilarating. It's clear Dylan has a rare gift for channeling sublime lyrics straight from the source; it is equally clear the divine messenger was a jerk. I kept thinking of the undeserving Mozart in *Amadeus*. Rough, tattered, blazing like a million suns, a rocket lifting off, this is an unforgettable portrait of a young artist. And the model for every rock bio since.

By D.A. Pennebaker
1967
96 min

Netflix
Amazon

Bounce

Who are these guys, the beefy ones standing at the gates of nightclubs and discos deciding who gets in? Are they as beautiful as the beautiful people they control? I never tire of seeing what really happens behind the scenes, or of hearing about what really goes into other people's occupations, and with this documentary I now know more about bouncers than I thought possible. For a bit of drama, there's an opening at a hot club, so we follow a few wannabees who hope to get the job. I was rooting for the meek giant who lived with his mom. It's a satisfying journey into a world you often cross but never see.

By Steven Cantor
2000
71 min

Netflix
Amazon

Bowling for Columbine

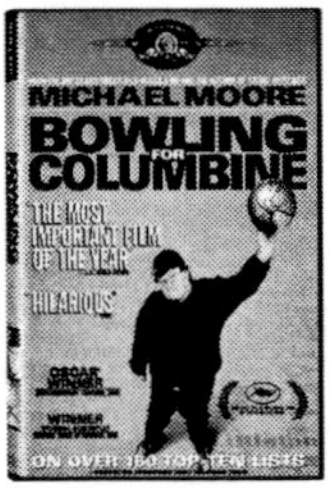

Michael Moore searches America (and Canada) for an answer to the question of why there are so many gun murders in the US. As a card-carrying, gun-toting NRA member, Moore reveals this quest to be more complex than you'd might expected. Always the coyote trickster, Moore investigates with great entertainment, and does here what he does best, pressing hard when people try to squirm out of honest answers. For a subject that should be ponderously serious and somber, this is a subtle, surreal and funny trip, and one that can change your mind.

By Michael Moore
2002
120 min

Netflix
Amazon

A Brief History of Time

This won't help you with physics, like the book did, but it will give you a powerful portrait of what a brain trapped in a withering body can still accomplish. Astrophysicist Stephen Hawking's ability to imagine the universe is matched only by his disheartening disability to do the most ordinary activity, including talking. His life is amazing; this film quite inspiring.

By Errol Morris
1992
80 min

Amazon

Brother's Keeper

Four elderly brothers share a dairy farm in the boonies of upper New York state. They are barely smarter than their cows, with some kind of genetic dim-wittedness. Without grooming skills, or reason to care, they soon are left alone in their muddy and filthy shack by their neighbors. Until one of the brothers dies. The older brother is charged with murdering him by suffocation as a mercy killing. There is no evidence – other than two of the brothers' own confessions to the police. But they retract those soon enough. Kind of. Their intelligence seems to fluctuate by whim. This story is about the subtle degrees of mental illness and what is disability (can you run a real farm for 40 years if you are retarded?), and the reach or overreach of law and its cold justice. Mostly you want to know, did the accused brother kill his brother to relieve him of his pain? An honest murder mystery. I liked it because I realized that if I were the cops I would not know what was fair.

By Joe Berlinger
1992
105 min

Netflix
Amazon

Buena Vista Social Club

Bands and concerts easily lend themselves to documentaries; they've got a built in soundtrack. This one follows the rediscovery of forgotten Cuban musicians as they make a new best-selling album. What works is the insight it provides to contemporary Cuba.

By Wim Wenders
1999
101 min

Netflix
Amazon

Burden of Dreams

One of the great films about filmmaking and artistic obsession (the other is *Heart of Darkness*). This film captures director Werner Herzog going quietly insane in the Amazon jungle while making his equally insane movie *Fitzcarraldo*. Herzog gradually becomes the very fictional character his movie is about, an obsessed madman determined to drag a riverboat over a mountain. (RK)

By Les Blank
1992
95 min

Amazon

Cane Toads: An Unnatural History

An offbeat, kinky, tongue-in-cheek celebration of the monstrous cane toad invasion of Australia and of the people who love the poisonous creatures and those who hate them. A nature film with attitude.

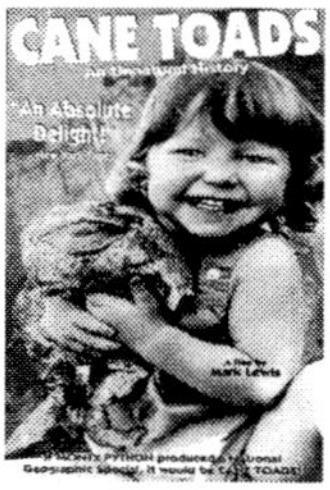

By Mark Lewis
1987
47 min

Netflix
Amazon

China: Beyond the Clouds

A million stories unfold in Lijiang, a picturesque historic town in the mountains of southwest China. This 4-hour tale follows four local families over several years as their lives twist, turn, deepen, intermingle, and blossom. Their openness is uncharacteristically candid for rural China; a tribute to veteran documentarian Phil Agland. The universal fears and dreams of a vast continent are condensed into a tightly edited few hours of subtitled witness. So intimate is this view of Chinese life that it is close to anthropology. Highly recommended.

1994
115 min

$40
Item #51749
National Geographic online store

Chuck Jones: Extremes and in Betweens

A lightweight biography of the guy who developed Bugs Bunny, Daffy Duck, Porky Pig, Roadrunner and the Warner Brothers style of slapstick cartoons. But that's not why this is worth seeing. On the special features menu on the DVD is a short tutorial by Chuck Jones on his rules of animation, illustrated by brilliant clips from his cartoon shorts. These spots quickly give you the best short course in classic comic animation you'll ever find. It's no more than 10 minutes but it's revelatory.

By Margaret Selby
2000
90 min

Netflix
Amazon

The Civil War

The most remarkable aspect of this most remarkable documentary is the emotional weight it carries. Comprised almost solely of slow passes across old black and white still photos (now known as a Ken Burns move) this expertly narrated film makes you weep and cringe and sail with deep understanding. It reordered my notion of the deepest scar (the largest war ever) on this continent. At 11 hours it's a long journey, but well worth it. It is hard to watch this series and not come to see it as *your* view of the Civil War. And it changed the language of documentary filmmaking, too.

By Ken Burns
1990
680 min

Netflix
Amazon

Civilization

Civilization as seen through the eyes of art and architecture. While art is the narrow focus, the vista in Kenneth Clark's view is as vast as 2,000 years of western history. The continuity of this long-view is a treat. I can't think of any other factual video with an equal span of attention.

By Michael Gill and Peter Montagnon
1969
5 volumes

Amazon

Colonial House

The premise is familiar now. Send a modern family into the past and make them live with only the tools and resources available centuries ago. In this case, the modern Americans are sent to live in the summer of 1628, on a forested island off of Maine. Their task: build a new world colony (20 people strong) that can both survive and pay back its investors in England. Life is pretty grungy. Two families to a room; no outhouses. This is the third in a series of living history documentaries (see *1900 House* and *Frontier House*) – only now they have fewer tools. Of the three programs this is the best, in part because of the reality show-like drama and bickering between the colonists. Cameras record every detail as the pudgy newcomers scrounge for food, learn how to farm Indian corn, all the while slowly starving, and assuming appropriate roles such as indentured servants with astounding ease. Who knew how easy devolution was? Like the hit TV series *Survivor*, it's about how primeval people get when survival is at stake. But unlike *Survivor*, there's historical logic, authentic rituals, and significant meaning in their test. My kids, both young and teenage, are addicted to these series. If I had to choose one, I'd start with this one, the 8-hour *Colonial House*.

By Nick Brown
2004
480 min

Netflix
Amazon

Cool & Crazy

Mild-mannered Norwegian bachelors living in a tiny fishing village north of the Arctic Circle find companionship and meaning in life by singing -- always singing – especially in their local male choir. It's fish, sing, or leave. Hoping to become world famous they travel to the depressingly polluted Russian industrial town of Murmansk to give a concert. It's a lovely film about how one's spirit can soar even when constrained by a dying small town. The title refers ironically to mild hopes and quiet lives of these bachelors of ice. Their music, surprisingly spiritual, fills the screen.

By Knut Erik Jensen
2001
89 min

Netflix
Amazon

Cosmos

Although it is now 25 years old, Carl Sagan's *Cosmos* still warrants viewing. I watched it again recently and it captured me. I've found no better orientation to the visible heavens and our small place in the universe than this 13-part series, now conveniently housed in one boxed DVD set. Most of the science is still valid, and Sagan's explanations and astronomical insights have yet to be exceeded for clarity and wit. When a student begins to wonder "where are we?" and asks other big questions, these are the disks to slide into the player.

By Carl Sagan
1980
780 min

GreenCine
Amazon

The Cruise

An unforgettable portrait of a truly original human being who happens to give tours of New York City on a double decker bus. The hero, Timmy "Speed" is either mentally ill or one of the most profound living poets. Or both. You can't tell. For sure, here is someone who "thinks different." By the end you get to see cities, society, the whole world in his offbeat, zany way, and it's a real kicker. The tour is worth repeating several times.

By Bennett Miller
1998
76 min

Amazon

Crumb

This has to be the most honest portrait of an artist ever. Robert Crumb, the 60's underground comic genius, is revealed in all his pathetic neuroses and glorious brilliance. The tipping point is being introduced to his eccentric family which suddenly explains all.

By Terry Zwigoff
1994
109 min

Netflix
Amazon

Dark Days

By Marc Singer
2000
88 min

Amazon
Netflix

The urban legend about cities of homeless living underground in the neglected corridors of New York City's subways was partly true. For about a decade in the 80s, a colony of extremely resourceful hobos built shelters in an underground section of Penn-Central railroad beneath New York. They had stolen electricity and a few even had cold running water; many worked outside as can collectors or street vendors and rifled garbage for uneaten restaurant food. This film documents their routines, their squabbles with each other, and their fight with the city to keep their plywood homes, filled with TVs, beds, and mini-kitchens. It's a fight they lost. Homelessness, like everything else in life, is not uniform. These folks were exceptionally resourceful and ambitious, and the story follows them up as they leave their eccentric handmade homes to acquire subsidized housing.

Destinos • French in Action

$450
52 30 minute parts
12 DVDs
www.learner.org

Destinos is a highly-evolved language learning program based on watching a soap opera – in Spanish. It consists of 52 half-hour segments of a detective mystery which was filmed in 5 countries on 3 continents. You start off with no Spanish and very rapidly become sucked into a long Spanish telenovela. The story is cleverly designed to steadily incorporate more sophisticated terms, so that by the 52nd show you can understand nearly everything in the first show. And then you start over. The first time around you won't understand much, the second time you watch the series you'll get half, and by the third you should comprehend most.

There is also a 52-part series for learning French called *French in Action*. I knew zero French, yet I was amazed how far I got so quickly merely by watching and responding to this series of ever deepening complexity. In *French in Action* you get a wild-haired French professor gesturing emphatically to convey weird French grammar, while cute little clips from French movies repeat a phrase in many voices so you can get used to hearing it spoken live.

Almost any library system in America will have these tapes; they are also frequently shown on public TV, sometimes on a few nights to facilitate home taping; they can be purchased (very expensively) on VHS or DVD, or they can also be viewed for free on the web at the url here.
Streaming video: www.learner.org/resources/series83.html or /series75.html

Devil's Playground

The riddle of how the Amish can maintain their population growth while choosing to live a stoic lifestyle in the middle of 21st century America is explored in this incredibly fascinating and brilliant documentary. When Amish reach 16 years old, they take off their hats and bonnets and immerse themselves into contemporary America with all its temptations, before deciding whether to join the puritanical Amish church once and for all. Many Amish teens delve deep into sex, drugs, and rock and roll (Amish parties are legendary and filmed here) never to return home, and to be eternally shunned by their large families. But an amazing 90% of Amish kids put beer and drug binges behind them and take up their horse and buggy. The films follows the excruciating decisions of Amish teens wavering on the edge between these extremes, and allows viewers to enter into the Amish mindset through its youth, and to see modernity in a different light.

By Lucy Walker
2002
77 min

Netflix
Amazon

Divine Horsemen

A 1950s capture of voodoo rituals in Haiti, created by Maya Deren, an experimental filmmaker. Because she was an initiate of voodoo, this film became an influential work of visual anthropology. It's value to me is in its rare portrayal of voodoo practice prior to becoming well known outside of Haiti.

By Lonard Forest
1985
52 min

Amazon

Dogtown and Z-Boys

You wouldn't expect a documentary about the slacker origins of skateboarding culture to hold your attention for more than 10 minutes, but *Dogtown and Z-boys* certainly does. It unleashes a steady stream of surprises, beginning with a small band of juvenile delinquents and outcast school kids who were so downtrodden they were kicked out of good waves in Santa Monica California. They then began to surf dorky skateboards. Soon they were amusing themselves with breaking into vacant backyard swimming pools and "taking on air" with zany skateboard antics and a lot of attitude. How this small-time obsession became an international sport, entertainment and merchandising complex is the rest of this amazing and well-made story. I consider it a key document of contemporary American culture.

By Stacy Peralta
2002
90 min

Netflix
Amazon

The Elegant Universe

A crash course in string theory -- the possible theory of everything. Fast-paced, crammed with high-street graphics and the best visualizations money can buy, this four-part Nova series does a fantastic job of making sense of something which inherently doesn't make sense -- as everyone in this show will tell you. Great pains are taken to keep things as simple as the honor of physicists will allow, and the host Brian Greene, physicist and author of the book of the same title, offers state-of-the-art explanations for weird ideas. I learned a whole lot. It's the best science teaching format yet.

By Joseph McMaster and Julia Cort
2003
180 min

Netflix
Amazon

F for Fake

Orson Welles was both a filmmaker and a stage magician and he uses all his visual and mental sleight-of-hand tricks in his free-form essay on the nature of lies and fakery. Primarily a portrait of an infamous art forger, it also features an interview with that other notorious faker (barely known at the time), Clifford Irving. (RK)

By Orson Welles
1976
85 min

Amazon

The Farm: Life Inside Angola Prison

A straight-on view of the legendary lifers' prison on an old slave plantation in Louisiana, where few leave alive. It's more honest than the TV fictional show *OZ* in that here some lifers find truth and happiness inside. Depicts the hell inside (I'll be good, I promise) and of course stirs up outrage (expected) but what I find worth recommending is the inspiration it plants as you see humans blossom in the most inhumane place.

By Jonathan Stack
and Liz Garbus
1998
100 min

Amazon

Films of Charles and Ray Eames

Their ingenious *Powers of Ten* film which zips you through the universe in ten-fold scale jumps is justly famous. Not as well known are their other short films which exhibit their pioneering sensibility (now mainstream): the marriage of technology and design. Try the Eames' short ode to toy trains, a review of their early industrial-chic home, and a *Mathematics Peep Show*, among others. All reward re-watching.

5 Volumes

Amazon

The Filth and the Fury

Julien Temple's surprisingly smart look at both the Sex Pistols and the birth of British punk. Using archival footage and contemporary interviews with the surviving band members, what emerges is less about the Pistols themselves than about one of those unique moments when you can feel pop culture shift under your feet. A surprise is the depth of feeling that comes out when John Lydon (Johnny Rotten) talks about Sid Vicious's death. (RK)

By Julien Temple
2000
108 min

Netflix
Amazon

Fire on the Mountain

In the pre-dawn of WWII, an ambitious outdoorsman convinces President Roosevelt to fund an elite army corp who are expert in mountain skills – to compliment US water and amphibious forces. They round up all the ski bums, mountain climbers and wilderness die-hards in America, long before such activities were mainstream. Among those who respond to this call is Sierra Club founder-to-be David Brower. The soldiers camp and train in Colorado, near the then unknown Aspen. They develop the snowmobile, the snow cat, early versions of modern camping, and modern ski techniques. Then off to the Alps in Italy where the US mountain unit defeats Nazi troops in a key mountain battle. Then they return to the US to invent the ski industry, Nike shoes, and run most of the ski resorts in the West. What holds all this together is the intense camaraderie of these outdoor fanatics. As one old soldier said, "This wasn't an Army unit. It was a fraternity."

By George and Beth Gage
1996
72 min

Netflix
Amazon

The Fog of War

Strictly a talking head -- this one of Robert McNamara, considered the chief strategist of the Vietnam War as he recounts his personal history of how the war began. There are many lessons to be had from his belated candor as an insider; the one I took away reflects the title of the documentary: not only was the public kept ignorant of all that was going on, but even the brass in charge did not fully agree on or understand what was happening: thus the fog of war. And 10 other lessons as well.

By Errol Morris
2003
107 min

Netflix
Amazon

Gates of Heaven

Errol Morris's 1978 documentary about pet cemeteries is so much more than that. Wrapped in layers of pathos, humor, and surprising candor, the film goes beyond mere novelty and becomes an examination of the power of love and the nature of life. (RK)

By Errol Morris
1978
85 min

Amazon

Ghengis Blues

What a wonderful adventure. A blind blues singer in San Francisco hears some strange music on a shortwave radio, and tracks it down as Tuvan throatsinging. It sounds like a whistle and a groan at the same time, and most people can't believe it comes from one human mouth. Our hero, Paul Pena, not only learns how to do it by reinventing it sitting in his home, he also learns Tuvan language by translating English to Russian to Tuvan in Braille! He then winds up getting invited to perform in the first Tuvan throatsinging contest since such contests were allowed after the breakup of the Soviet Union. (Tuva, near Mongolia, is a small autonomous republic within the Russian Federation.) The film starts here as it follows this blind black man into the heart of Mongolia to try to win a horse by groaning two notes at once while singing the Tuvan national anthem. It's a wild and strange trip.

By Roko Belic
1999
88 min

Netflix
Amazon

Gimme Shelter

Woodstock gone bad. With poor planning this free Rolling Stones concert in 1969 spun out of control. Given the rampant drug highs, a quarter million kids, the presence of the Hells Angles as guards, and the Rolling Stones own "Sympathy for the Devil," it is amazing that only one person was murdered in the chaos. This classic documentary offers two things: footage of the young Rolling Stones in concert at their peak, and a lesson of the underbelly of self-organization – when anarchy takes over.

By David Maysles, Albert Maysles, and Charlotte Zwerin
1970
91 min

Netflix
Amazon

Hands on a Hard Body

In the South of the US, where getting a new truck is a type of rebirth, there is a little-known contest whereby a truck dealer, as a publicity stunt, will offer a new truck to the person who can keep his/her hand on a truck the longest. Typically these endurance tests run 80-90 hours, or almost 4 days. During that time, contestants must stand awake, with at least one hand on the vehicle. Each hopeful is absolutely sure they will win (what does it take besides desire?) and the candid stories of their desires are wonderful. As the hours pass into days, fatigue and insanity take over so the outcome of the test is completely unpredictable. This small gem of a film is a testament to the indomitable spirit and outright brittleness of the human mind.

By S.R. Bindler
1997
85 min

Amazon

Hearts of Darkness

A film is like an invasion. Vietnam War's most memorable film, *Apocalypse Now*, like the war itself, nearly did in its creators. Francis Ford Cuppola's wife filmed the director as his project sank deeper and deeper into sheer, irretrievable chaos. This is a strange case where the movie about the movie is just as good as the movie.

By Eleanor Coppola
1991
96 min

Amazon

Heavy Metal Parking Lot

On the evening of May 31, 1986, a pair of aspiring documentary filmmakers took their video equipment to the Capital Center arena outside Washington, DC, and filmed teenagers arriving for a concert by the British heavy metal thudmasters Judas Priest. Jeff Krulik and John Heyn scooped up a pure slab of teenage wasteland by simply asking dumb questions ("Does anybody here do air guitar") and recording while increasingly sauced teens wheeled around in their orange cars and got "ready to rawk!" Like Jane Goodall peeking through the leaves at the chimps, the filmmakers captured an amazing anthropological slice of life, complete with bad hair, bad teeth, bare chests and semi-articulate babbling. *Heavy Metal Parking Lot* is a short work, only 15 minutes long, but it's an ingenious masterpiece. (JD)

By Jeff Krulik and John Heyn
1986
15 min

Amazon

Hell House

A weird form of evangelism that is slowly gaining among fundamentalists. Churches in the midwest construct vast "hell houses" to scare visitors to Jesus. Originally begun as a response to Halloween haunted houses, these elaborate stagings, crammed with theatrical effects and high-school actors on October 31, try to outdo each other in their ultra-realistic depiction of sin and horror. This documentary follows one church as they embark on another year of creatively presenting depravity – a labyrinth of rooms each seeded with a different sin (suicide, drug addiction, prostitution) realistically reenacted. Innocent kids scare themselves sick by how realistic they've made their own hell. The film works because it is sympathetic to those possessed by their enemy, and because it doesn't overdo the obvious irony that hell houses are so spooky in concept that they scare in the wrong direction. On the other hand, nobody creates such amazing haunted houses like they do.

By George Ratliff
2001
86 min

Netflix
Amazon

Hoop Dreams

The thrill of a really great factual is you don't know how it is going to end. Here we follow young inner-city kids trying to escape their circumstances by making it big in basketball. We see how hard it is, and how big the dream can be. I came to root for them as if they were family.

By Steve James (II)
1994
170 min

Amazon

How To Draw a Bunny

A pointed film about a most peculiar artist – an artist too peculiar even for the New York art crowd. Ray Johnson had as much talent as Andy Warhol (a friend and colleague) but he *really* didn't want money or fame. He just wanted to make mail art and rubber stamps and to amuse himself at home with whimsical and sly collages. (A goofy kilroy-is-here scribble bunny became his signature.) Soon, like Picasso, or a naive folk artist, everything in his grasp became art. Real artists grokked his stuff – if they ever got to see it, which few did. So he came by reputation to be the most famous unknown artist in America and then mysteriously disappeared. He left behind a huge master collage – one clue pointing to the next in a complex recursive joke – which turned out to be his life. In a delicious way I really enjoy, this documentary itself became an intregal part of his grand collage to keep us guessing.

By John W. Walter
2002
90 min

Netflix
Amazon

Incident at Oglala

An engrossing legal and societal drama based on a court case involving American Indian activist Leonard Peltier, convicted for allegedly killing two FBI agents and another Native American in a shoot-out on the Pine Ridge Reservation in South Dakota in June 1975. The film gives us a vivid picture of the desperately poor Indian reservations of South Dakota, where ramshackle houses prevail, unemployment rates soar, and the landscape can reveal a magnificent vista in one direction or an unconscious drunk in another. *Incident at Oglala* pulls apart court testimony, highlights discrepancies and reveals that a century after the Massacre at Wounded Knee, Native Americans are still often treated like bad dogs. (JD)

By Michael Apted
1992
90 min

Netflix
Amazon

Joseph Campbell and the Power of Myth

Proving that even an interview format can succeed if done with passion, this famous set of conversations between Joseph Campbell and Bill Moyers on the power of myths still delivers a very powerful punch.

By Bill Moyers
1988
360 min

Netflix
Amazon

Junkyard Wars

The TV show said to be the most commonly recorded on TiVo is the hackers' special, *Junkyard Wars*. Two teams of tinkerers race against each other to construct a working submarine, or an airplane, or a cannon, or deep-sea diving gear, all assembled from scrap found in a junkyard, and all built within a day and a half. That both sides usually succeed at some level (although only one side wins) is the first surprise of this TV series. More amazing is the easy lesson in physics and engineering each episode brings. By watching how a pump is cobbled together from motorscooter tires, one gets a visceral sense of how a pump works. By watching how geeks think around impossible obstacles, one catches the confidence to tackle an impossible project. They are educational enough that some science classes show them.

Episodes available, for example:
Junkyard Wars: Cannons Video #187435
Junkyard Wars: Flying Machines Video #187450

$6
The Discovery Store
shopping.discovery.com/AltHome.html

Jupiter's Wife

A sophisticated New York City filmmmaker meets a homeless woman in Central Park, and finds her to be unusually smart, vivacious, and seemingly happy to camp year-round with her dogs. How does she get by with so much enlightened contentment? It's soon obvious the attractive woman is certifiably crazy, operating on another plane of reality. Voices tell her she is Jupiter's wife. But rather than flee, as any sane person would do, the filmmaker decides to unravel her story. He does this by taking her irrational claims as coded messages which he learns to interpret from her outrageous clues. He uses his investigative skills in New York to piece together her submerged life, and he then tells the fascinating story she is no longer capable of telling. It is a remarkable achievement. Although he tries to help her, in the end she returns to the park. But the film completely changed my understanding of what the voices say to the afflicted: they are a code that tries to explain. In the middle of the film you'll want to bail because you are completely focused on someone's derangements, but its worth hanging through to the conclusion as the filmmaker completes his amazing decipherment.

By Michel Negroponte
1995
78 min

Netflix
Amazon

Keep the River on Your Right

As he nears old age, a New York City artist decides to revisit the adventures of his youth in distant lands. In the 1950s, while on an art fellowship, Tobias Schneebaum walked alone and unguided into the Peruvian Amazon rainforest to make first contact with some Indian headhunters. He shed his clothes and old ways and went native with them. But after his clan raided a neighboring tribe, murdered the villagers, and then ate their enemies in a victory feast – and he ate too, he decided to return. Later he ended up collecting the art of headhunters in New Guinea, where he lived with another tribe who were also cannibalistic, and subsequently fell in love with, and become partners with, one of the hunters. Forty years later he is persuaded, despite having an artificial hip, to leave his now well-worn routines in NYC to see if he can find the tribesmen in the Amazon and New Guinea again. He gets them to talk about their former eating habits. This is a complex weave of the weirdness of nostalgia, the subtleties of cross cultural communication, and the attraction of Otherness.

By David Shapiro II and Laurie Shapiro
2000
94 min

Netflix
Amazon

Kestrel's Eye

Nature photography doesn't come much purer. Filmed over several years from and in a church tower in Norway, this unadorned film of hawk life, from birth to death, is seen from the birds' eye view, with no human narration. Extreme filmmaking, extreme birdness.

By Mikael Kristersson
1999
89 min

Netflix
Amazon

Koyaanisqatsi

The title is a Hopi Indian word meaning "life out of balance." Created between 1975 and 1982, the narrative-free documentary is a strange and beautiful visual feast featuring hypnotic images illustrating civilization's impact on Earth. With its haunting score by Philip Glass and stunning cinematography, *Koyaanisqatsi* takes the viewer on a wild flight from the tranquil deserts of the United States, through verdant planes and forests to cacophonous urban areas. The pace accelerates as the music and images show how modern life corrodes both planet and soul. (JD)

By Godfrey Reggio
1983
87 min

Netflix
Amazon

The Last Waltz

Not another band movie! No, not just another band movie. Mixing performance footage from The Band's last concert together with interviews, director Martin Scorcese reinvents the concert film, bringing to it all the cinematic flair he used on movies such as *Raging Bull* and *Goodfellas.* (RK)

By Martin Scorsese
1978
117 min

Netflix
Amazon

Lessons of Darkness

At the end of the Gulf War (no, the other one, back in the early 90s) German director and mad documentarian Werner Herzog went to Kuwait, to record the spectacularly burning oil fields, the families of torture victims and the weapons of war themselves. In the film, we enter from high above, and spend a good part of the film there, like God looking down and wondering why part of the world suddenly looks like Bosch's image of Hell. (RK)

By Werner Herzog
1992
50 min

GreenCine
Amazon

The Life of Birds

Of all of David Attenborough's famous and fabulous surveys of life, this one on the life of birds is his best – perhaps because Attenborough loved birds the most. His look at winged creatures is quirky, intelligent, deep, and memorable. It nicely serves as a brilliant short course in ornithology, or as a mesmerizing way to keep restless young humans tamed for hours because he reveals one amazing thing after another. You can find nature films round the clock on cable; this series is simply in a class by itself, worth re-watching many times. Extreme Birds is how I think of it.

By David Attenborough
1998
540 min.

Netflix
Amazon

The Life of Mammals

I've long marveled at how David Attenborough's films overshadow all other nature documentaries, of which there are many. Attenborough's *Life of Mammals* is no exception. First, he organizes the mammalian world by big ideas (Chisellers, Opportunists, Return to Water, etc.). Then, he is there – right next to the animal as he expounds – transmitting vibes in a live 220 volt connection. Finally, he elects to show details of mammal life that are quirky, not usually seen, and always with a point. This kind of deep intelligence and love for his subjects rewards re-viewing. This 10-part series (about 9 hours) is a family favorite.

By David Attenborough
2002
200 min

Netflix
Amazon

Looking for Richard

While preparing a production of Richard III, actor Al Pacino and his cast ask "Why do we perform Shakespeare anymore?" Scenes are ripped apart and history is dissected. A great glimpse of raw creativity by a stellar acting ensemble. (RK)

By Al Pacino
1996
118 min

Amazon

Lumiere & Co.

To commemorate the 100th anniversary of the Lumiere brothers' first movie, forty directors from around the world are invited to use one of the brothers' handcranked cameras to make an original 52-second film (the length of the Lumieres' original reels). The results from these modern artists range from pedestrian to stunning, with David Lynch, Peter Greenawy and Alain Corneau turning in especially memorable sequences. (RK)

By David Lynch
1995
88 min

Netflix
Amazon

Mein Krieg

Home movies shot by six different Nazi youth as they marched toward the Russian front as German soldiers in World War II, some of it in color. They narrate the footage later as older men. What you get is the everyday details of their life then, and how they saw the world, what they found important, or new, and what they were thinking. It smells true.

By Harriet Eder and Thomas Kufus
1991
90 minutes

Amazon

Microcosmos

It begins as a small nod to the insects in your backyard, but soon becomes a wide-opened window into a previously unknown microcosm of insect-dom. How is it possible we've never seen this world before with this clarity? With scarce narration this better-than-usual nature film is more poem than documentary. Works for kids. Produced by the same Frenchman who later did *Winged Migration*.

By Claude Nuridsany and Marie Perennou
1996
80 min

Amazon

Nanook of the North

One of the first film documentaries in history, and still unrivaled for clarity and amazement. Shows how Eskimo (Inuit) survived in a Mars-like environment with traditional ways.

By Robert J. Flaherty
1922
79 min

Netflix
Amazon

The Natural History of the Chicken

An offbeat look at chickens and the people who love chickens way too much.

By Mark Lewis
2000
60 min

GreenCine
Amazon

Notebook on Cities & Clothes

A meditation on the power of images, place and the loss of the self in a digital culture. This cinematic journal by Wim Wenders centers on Japanese clothing designer Yoji Yamamoto, and explores how what we wear can define us as individuals. (RK)

By Wim Wenders
1989
81 min

Netflix
Amazon

Okie Noodling

You simply have to see this one to believe it. A weekend fisherman in Oklahoma crawls along the bottom of a creek, head submerged under the muddy water, wiggling his fingers in dark holes and crevices. When a huge catfish hiding in the muck swallows his hand, the man yanks the 70 pound beast up out of the water, suckered to his fist. It's call noodling and your average Okie redneck thinks this foolishness gives rednecks a bad name. The noodlers think its the only fair way to fish. The filmmakers decide to hold the first national Noodling Contest for cash, which brings to light more noodlers than anyone knew about. After a while, sticking your hand into a dark underwater hole to let a monstrous fish bite it seems like a perfectly reasonable way to fish.

By Bradley Beesley
2001
57 min

Netflix
Amazon

Project Greenlight

Should the desire to go to film school ever seize you, buy this 4 disc CD set instead. You'll learn about as much and save many thousands of dollars. HBO sponsored a contest where the newbie winner – selected from 10,000 entrants after intense auditions – gets to direct and film their first-time screenplay. Of course HBO gets to film *them* as they thrash and burn. Naturally the documentary about the making of is better than the first time film, called Stolen Summer, also included. (I actually liked it.) There's plenty of drama in the 13-part "making of it" – back-stabbing, flameouts, hysteria, betrayals, and the uncertainty of whether the final film will be watchable. As a bonus, after 10 hours of this insider's view, you'll know how films are really made, and you'll be certain you could do better.

Starring Ben Affleck and Matt Damon
2001
500 min

Netflix
Amazon

Project Grizzly

A Canadian outdoorsman who fancies himself a survival expert crosses the wrong side of a grizzly bear. The grizzly begins to attack him, but our hero stares the bear down, nose to snout, inches apart. In that moment of eye contact, our hero has a cosmic connection with the bear and vows to return to meet grizzly face to face again. But he's no fool, so he decides to invent a grizzly-proof suit. For the next seven years he spends hundreds of thousands of dollars developing the whackiest series of full-body armour outfits, each one stronger, stranger, and more invincible, but less mobile. In a demented logic he tests the suits by having speeding trucks knock him down or by swinging half ton blocks of concrete into his head. In his obsession to face grizzly he becomes a deranged captain Ahab, and you are both horrified, uplifted and transfixed as you watch him sink. It's captured for real; you couldn't make this one up.

By Peter Lynch
1997
72 min

Amazon

Pumping Iron

Filmed more than 25 years ago, long before weight lifting was considered healthy and fashionable, this dramatic 16mm film introduced the world to professional muscle men. These misshapen guys were assumed to be outright freaks, whose fandom was fringe and tiny. But I was surprised how much appreciation for bodybuilding as art and sport I gained in just one watching. But most fascinating is the film's focus on an unknown young champion from Austria, Arnold Schwarzenegger, whose ambitions and manipulations are naked and unbounded. Looking back now from his later destiny as governor of California and international movie star, this classic documentary is doubly mesmerizing.

By George Butler II and Robert Fiore
1976
85 min

Netflix
Amazon

Revolution OS

Two themes that normally don't intersect in true films come together surprisingly well in this simple documentary: history and the last five minutes. *Revolution OS* explores the significance of trendy open-source software by going deep into its short history, acting as if open-source technology was a world-changing event of such magnitude that everyone will someday demand to know how it began. Which they probably will. Here is the film they will show later this century. The stress is on the political, not the technical. No drama, either; just clean geek history of a big idea when it started out small.

By J.T.S. Moore
2002
86 min

Netflix
Amazon

Rick Steves' Travel Skills

I rely on Rick Steves' masterly command of travel minutia to guide me in Europe. This guy spends 4 months there every year keeping his advice updated in his expanding line of eponymous books. Rick has the drill down perfectly, and he has a real gift for teaching what he knows. Yet as great as his books are, the very best way to get educated in traveling Europe with ease and grace is to watch his short course in *Travel Skills*. I am a hardened veteran traveler and I picked up some great tips. If you are just starting out to Europe, I can't recommend this enough.

Once sold as a separate tape, this video is now packaged as part of a longer DVD which also includes a quick and lively video tour of Germany and the Swiss Alps by Rick Steves himself.

By Rick Steves
4 hours

Ricksteves.com

$20 *from travelstore.ricksteves.com/catalog/index.cfm?fuseaction=product&theParentId=16&id=108*

Ring of Fire: An Indonesian Odyssey

The best travel documentary series ever made. For ten years two brothers lived in, adventured throughout, and mastered the islands of Indonesia. They delve into this truly esoteric culture with reckless enthusiasm and true love. And they film a lot of bizarre events. This is travel as art.

By Lorne and Lawrence Blair
1999
240 min

Amazon

Rivers and Tides

One of the best films about art, by one of our best living artists. Drift in and out of the dreams of Andy Goldsworthy as he summons a mesmerizing cornucopia of temporary monuments – an arc of icicles, a train of flowers, a hive of sticks – from bits of leaves, twigs, rocks, ice and mud. He makes things you could easily make – if only you saw the world as he does. By the end of this beautifully lyrical film, you DO begin to share Goldsworthy mystical vision of a world swimming in energy and flows. More than anything else Goldsworthy celebrates childlike play, a playfulness which this films radiates. The most profound moments catch the artist despairing as his painstakingly constructed pieces fail before they are finished. Later he watches in boyish glee as they naturally fall apart. I feel angelic when I watch this.

By Thomas Riedelsheimer
2001
90 min

Netflix
Amazon

Roger & Me

More guerilla theater than a documentary, this is a road trip by trouble-maker Michael Moore as he chases down an unwanted interview with the remote head of General Motors. Moore resorts to a bag of tricks and subterfuge to dispense his political message on the way. The result is funny, infuriating, verbose, sly, arrogant and hilarious all at once. If you like to watch the little guy tweek the big guy, you'll like this.

By Michael Moore
1989
90 min

Netflix
Amazon

Rough Science

A very cool BBC series wherein the crafty producers take a bunch of scientists and technicians to a remote location and have them recreate sophisticated tools and inventions using only the primitive materials on hand. Vines, wood, bits of metal, shells. Here: make a clock (with bell), or a device to record sounds, or how about a camera, microscope, soap and sunblock; or go survey and map the island – using tools of your own construction. You don't know science until you can roll your own. This 10-part program is highly instructional because you get to see technology reduced to its essence – and because not everything works. The DVDs are expensive; fire up your TiVo to catch them on PBS; another new series begins this fall.

By Sarah Topalian and David Shulman
2002
90 min

Bullfrog

A vailable from Bullfrog Films, www.bullfrogfilms.com
(Ignore the ridiculous price of $890 for the 10-part series DVD on the website; Bullfrog offers an undisclosed "home use" price of $200 for the set or $25 each per tape of 10 or $65 per each of 3 DVDs. 800-543-3764)

Scratch

It ain't news that kids play the turntable as if it was a musical instrument but this fast-paced history of how DJ scratching was invented is pretty cool. Profiles of four famous "turntable-ists" give a clear picture of how remarkable their scratching skill is; they can essentially sing by deftly oscillating appropriate portions of several records. With fine detail the film reveals the scratchers extreme dedication to innovation, constant practice, and an obsessive knowledge of records. It's quite a trip, very geeky in many ways, but it increased my respect and admiration for this weird little achievement 1000%.

By Doug Pray
2001
92 min

Netflix
Amazon

The Shape of Life

This 8-part (4 DVD set) series is a National Science Foundation/PBS production that is the most taxonomic of any presentation I've seen. The *Shape of Life* addresses the 8 major categories of animal life -- phylum by phylum. Starts with sponges, heads toward round worms, and so on. You get the full diverse view of life -- all intelligently organized around a taxonomic framework (without the vocabulary), and expertly illustrated with great (mostly undersea) BBC-type footage. Despite the wonderful nature photography, the creators work really hard to convey the innovations offered by each phylum, and it succeeds. This series cured me of a rather vague notion of animal diversity, despite my work at All Species. I'd love to ingest the same mind-opening treatment for the plant world, as well as the other 3 kingdoms.

2002
480 min

Amazon

Silk Road

Even in Marco Polo's time the Silk Road between Europe and China wove through vast desert wildernesses and sparsely populated steppes. It was a tough and lonely journey then, and unlike most travels in 2004, it still is a journey through grand nothingness. Because it has always been so remote, the ruins of those ancient days lay near our modern touch now. One can still find bits of silk hundreds of years old fluttering in the sand at ruins on the old road. In 1979 the Chinese government and NHK, the Japanese TV station, teamed up to make a well-financed expedition to explore the Silk Road within the Chinese borders, and the resulting documentary remains the best orientation to what remains of that ancient route. The big surprise is the extent of Buddhism in the lands we now imagine as classically Islamic. Think of those Buddhists' statues in Afghanistan. At times this 12-hour (!) extravagant travelogue plods as slow as a Chinese propaganda movie, and the soundtrack is inexplicably scored by the new age celebrity musician Kitaro, but Central Asia is looming on the horizon as the political hot-spot of this new century, so better get your maps out as the caravan trudges along.

1990
600 min

Netflix
Amazon

Sing Faster

A quick look at the work of stage hands on the very elaborate set of the epic Wagner Ring Cycle opera. Stage hands are like sailors (all that rigging). These guys seem to date only ballerinas, and they endure long spells of boredom between intense physical coordination. The title of the film comes from their eternal desire to close the last act: "Come on, sing faster" they mutter. The best parts of this short peek behind the scenes are the interviews where stage hands give their New York street version of the convoluted plot of the Wagner operas playing endlessly around them.

By Jon Else
1999
60 min

Netflix
Amazon

The Sorrow and the Pity

On paper *The Sorrow and the Pity* sounds torturous: more than four hours of talking-head interviews in several languages, blended with wartime documentary footage and zipped up with the music of Maurice Chevalier. But don't run just yet. This epic account of France under the occupation of the Nazi regime during World War II is a humanist masterpiece, thanks to an artful assortment of film technique and pacing. Ophuls interviewed the residents of the French town of Clermont-Ferrand who remembered the Occupation, as well as various French, German, and British officials, local artists and farmers, as well as German army veterans. The result is a transcendent portrait of how real people conduct themselves under the most extreme circumstances. Ophuls constantly invites us to put ourselves in the position of each one of these people and ask: what would I have done in the same circumstances? (JD)

By Marcel Ophuls
1971
265 min

GreenCine
Amazon

Spellbound

An amazingly spellbinding drama. You follow a dozen elementary school students who memorize the dictionary and beyond, practicing for years at all waking hours in order to spell words they – and you! – have never heard of. Their ordinary parents are awestruck, the kids are driven, and the outcome is totally unpredictable. Only one kid will survive the National Spelling Bee. Will it be the one whose Indian parents have hired three foreign language coaches, or the girl whose dad does not even speak English? Or the boy with the stutter? It's a fantastic journey into a subculture that is uniquely American, yet invisible and marginal. Since you are on the edge of your seat most of the film, it even changes your ideas about spelling.

By Jeffrey Blitz
2002
97 min

Netflix
Amazon

Startup.com

Boy, did this documentary of a dot-com startup and meltdown resurrect old memories. It's been what, four years? Internet stock hysteria was so inflated that there are few families in America who were not touched by it in some way. Hundreds of thousands of urban workers had direct experience in this madness, but little knowledge of how the particulars worked. This fly-on-the-wall view of the birth and flameout of an Internet startup is the real thing, and should be prescribed as a catharsis if you ever owned stock in the last 5 years. Do you wonder where you pension money went? Watch this.

By Jehane Noujaim
2001
103 min

Netflix
Amazon

Survival Research Laboratories: Ten Years of Robotic Mayhem

Who wouldn't want to see machines destroy other machines? Long before *Battle Bots, Terminator* and the *Matrix* series, Mark Pauline and his collective of avant guarde engineers have been staging demolition derbies featuring custom built mechanical monsters. They spit fire, explode, squash metal, whack off parts and grind each other up – within feet of onlookers packed into a parking lot or highway underpass. The aim is to create danger and provoke the audience out of its passivity. This compendium of four past performances is the best of their influential grunge theater and robotic art.

By Jonathan Reiss
2004
60 min

Netflix
Amazon

Swimming to Cambodia

Spalding Gray's cleverly staged monologue is both a tall tale and a reflection on acting in *The Killing Fields*, the fall of Cambodia (and subsequent genocide) and his own search for spirituality. (RK)

By Jonathan Demme
1987
85 min

Netflix
Amazon

Theremin

Some lives need a movie. Russian inventor Leon Theremin created the world's first electronic instrument, and it bore his name. He was an outstanding success in the 1920s and 30s, but in the 40s, he disappeared. This film looks at Theremin's overlooked life and work, and reveals the reasons for his disappearance and brief reappearance in his 90s. Interviews include theremin virtuoso Clara Rockmore and synthesizer pioneer Robert Moog. (RK)

By Steven M. Martin
1995
82 min

GreenCine
Amazon

Thin Blue Line

A modern-day Rashamon, set in Texas. This version of the tale involves a real man, named Randall Adams, claiming innocence while stuck on death row. The film hypnotically plays out his alleged murder of a cop over and over, each time according to different witnesses, until the "evidence" of the crime collapses under the tainted weight of so many versions. This was a new form of nonfiction film and it helped free an innocent man from prison. How many films can claim that? (RK)

By Errol Morris
1988
103 min

Amazon

Touching the Void

This true film re-enacts a harrowing adventure by two mountaineers on a remote peak in the Andes, still unclimbed today. Near the top one climber with a badly broken leg disappears over the edge of a cliff in a storm, hangs by a single rope, but is thought to be dead, so the rope is cut. Miraculously the injured man falls into a deep crevasse, lives, and crawls out with his hands and rolls down a glacier and creeps back to camp almost dead on his elbows 6 days after they set out. Together with two stunt men, the two climbers re-live their nightmare by re-climbing the route and revealing what they were thinking the first time around. As an act of honesty, bravery and endurance, it's staggering to watch. At every junction you are sure, this is the end! But it isn't. In the climbing community this is considered one of the best mountaineering films ever.

By Kevin MacDonald
2003
106 min

Netflix
Amazon

Triumph of the Will

One of the most controversial films in cinematic history, as well as one of the most frightening and beautifully made. The subject is the spectacle of the 1934 session of Nazi Party Congress, at mass rallies involving thousands. The cinematography is gorgeous, the subjects are heroic. Critics brand *Triumph of the Will* a Nazi propaganda film that lionized butchers. True enough, and those charges had it banned for nearly 30 years. But a DVD version attempts to put the *Triumph of the Will* in its proper historical context by providing a substantial amount of material concerning the making of the film, including later interviews with Riefenstahl. The result is a critical look at a documentary that manages to capture a horrifying era through an extraordinary blend of inspired art, direction and cinematography. (JD)

By Leni Riefenstahl
1934
110 min

Netflix
Amazon

Troublesome Creek

A gentle, polite and very mid-western look at how a hard-working Iowa farm family loses their farm and sells it off in a mid-winter auction Sounds boring, but the film manages to make it dramatic and insightful. A real ticket into the deepest crevice of heartland America.

By Jeanne Jordan and Steven Ascher
1995
88 min

Amazon

Unzipped

The concept is simple. Reveal what really happens as a world-class couture designer develops, in fits and starts, his fall line. Show the factual side of a fashion show. The result is both hilarious and mesmerizing. Unexpectedly I came to appreciate fashion designers as artists, even though I have zero fashion sense.

By Douglas Keeve
1995
73 min

Netflix
Amazon

Up Series
7 Up, 14 Up, 21 Up, 28 Up, 35 Up, 42 Up

What started out as a British documentary exposing the role of class in a child's destiny has turned into one of the most satisfying works of cultural anthropology. It is now a showcase longitudinal study. Every seven years, starting at the age of seven, we visit the same group of children as they grow up, have dreams, are lost and remade, and in many cases see their lives take the unexpected turn as they age. Because each new film is created to be understood by itself, each recapitulates all the others before it, so there is a lot of repetition from issue to issue, but a lot missing if you only see the last one.

By Michael Apted
2004
576 min

Netflix
Amazon

Waco: The Rules of Engagement

This documentary has grown on me. At first I thought it a biased view of a minor argument between a rinky-dink kook and an edgy government agency which doesn't know how to deal with a messiah. The films reconstructs how in 1993 the US government burnt down (accidentally?) a commune of 74 men, women and children after an insane 2-month long siege. All dead were followers of David Koresh, a cultish pastor of a messianic Christianity, who stupidly, recklessly, selfishly (and criminally) put his entire commune in the line of fire and likely death. Yet it is clear that the childish behavior of the US government as it reacted to a bully was far more reckless, stupid and wrong than Koresh's. Over time this film didn't fade away as many activist films do. Rather it has only grown in import as the US has begun to deal with extreme religious believers elsewhere. The events of the standoff and incineration at the church in Waco shows that regardless of who is president, there's no return from hatred once you demonize the antagonist. This film includes revealing home videos made by the believers trapped inside, new aerial film of the crazy bombardment, and first-hand accounts of terrible misunderstandings. If your government hasn't enraged you in a while, try this film. Works for both lefties and right-wingers!

By William Gazecki
1997
136 min

Netflix
Amazon

Walking With...The Complete Collection

What if you could film dinosaurs on location, like in a nature documentary? That's what this four-hour BBC extravanaza does with advanced digital technology. The incredible footage in *Walking with Dinosaurs* is utterly convincing. Home movies of Ornithocheirus. As far as science can presently tell, this is what dinosaurs were like. From mating rituals, to tending their young; from chasing prey to fleeing from predators. These videos are better than any textbook: scientifically sound, technically astounding. Even better is *Walking with Prehistoric Beasts.* This sequel expands the variety of creatures brought back to digital life. You get saber tooth tigers, giant sloths, and a two-ton armadillo, among other extinct species – all with the same versimilitude of a convincing digital recreation. One continues to believe they were merely filmed. *Walking with Allosaurus* features one species of dino in depth. The "making of" portions for each film by the zoologists are just as educational . We watch these films quite often. *Walking with Dinosaurs* alone is worth four hours of your time.

2004
240 min each

Netflix
Amazon

The Way Things Go

This supremely demented documentary by two German artists presents a continuous chain reaction than runs for the length of the film. Old tires, ladders, shoes, flames and explosions trigger the next piece of precariously balanced junk. This art-piece is greatly appreciated by nerds for the amazing chemistry and physics required to keep self-generated chaos on track. Science teachers play the video for lessons in equilibrium and causation, while artists roll the film at parties for an irresistible and mesmerizing spectacle. I like it for the illustration of the never-ending chain reaction that seems to take over the world. A Mr. Wizard science demonstration that takes on its own life.

By Peter Fischli and David Weiss
1987
30 min

GreenCine
Amazon

When We Were Kings

This is the most popular documentary in print. I recently did a survey of industry awards, best-of-lists, and reviewer favorites: *When We Were Kings* was on more lists than any other documentary. It tells of the triumph of Muhammad Ali, the first global celebrity athlete. Even today he is probably the most famous athlete world-wide. The story of his rise from small time boxer Cassius Clay to draft resister, to poetry reader to world champ after a famous fight in Zaire, Africa would be entertaining in itself. But what puts this documentary over the top is the cast of characters – from Ali himself, to his antagonist (George Foreman), announcer (Howard Cosell), reporters (Norman Mailer), entourage (James Brown), promoters – all who loom way larger than life. If you were to write a Hollywood version of Ali's life and then try to cast actors to juice up the roles, you simply could not cast more outrageous people than the actual folks themselves – here forever documented with drama, intrigue, and plot twists.

By Leon Gast
1996
89 min

Netflix
Amazon

William Gibson: No Maps for these Territories

Science-fiction author William Gibson is locked inside a limo and driven around several cities while he muses improvisationally on the twilight between present and future. Pure talking-head, with a seat-belt. But the bizarre imprisonment gives a good dose of Gibson, who is often at his best in conversation.

By Mark Neale
2000
88 min

Netflix
Amazon

Winged Migration

Fly like a bird! You are a bird in flight, wing to wing with your feathered brethren as you fly south in this remarkable film. Shot over five years by training birds to fly alongside ultra light planes in locales around the world, this documentary magically immerses you into the bird dimension. Be the bird! Graceful and beautiful, and extremely satisfying. I found it an out-of-the body experience.

By Jacque Perrin
2003
98 min

Netflix
Amazon

Wonders of the African World

Most reports about Africa emphasize one of two well-worn themes: a) Africa's awesome natural environment, or b) its titillating variety of tribal life. This 6-hour video series illuminates a third, refreshing, little-seen dimension: African civilizations. Harvard professor Skip Gates narrates his very personal investigations into the overlooked black civilizations that blossomed on the African continent. Sometimes Gates is a little too full of himself, but other times his intensely idiosyncratic road show works perfectly in conveying the magic of ancient civilizations few Westerners are aware of. This video series is oddly better than any book about this overlooked subject – perhaps because the film succeeds in reflecting the tremendous oral and visual nature of these cultures. I had my mind changed.

By Henry Louis Gates Jr.
1999
6 hours

Amazon

Woodstock: 3 Days of Peace and Music

Some threshold was crossed at Woodstock in 1969 when half a million kids appeared out of nowhere to govern themselves and listen to their favorite bands in the rain. The music (pretty great), the vibes, and the expectations and hope of this outburst of optimism are all captured in this remarkable film – which everyone agrees was much better than being there. The dreams of two decades are encapsulated into 4 hours.

By Michael Wadleigh
1970
228 min

Netflix
Amazon

World War II: The Lost Color Archives

It's eerie how the simple addition of color can utterly transform our notions of the past. The restoration of color to World War II takes it from a remote, starkly defined monument into an immediate, vibrant, contemporary experience. It's at once more shocking and more beautiful. Enough experimental color footage (digitally restored) was filmed by US, German, and Japanese photographers to provide this amazing three-hour account of the war from all sides. This is how the participants of Europe and the Pacific saw it. Their words and letters form the narration for this British product. Disturbing though it is, this is the version that one wants to remember of the last world war.

1999
165 minutes

Netflix
Amazon